MUHAMMAD ALI

# MUHAMMAD ALI / BY MAGNUM PHOTOGRAPHERS

### INTRODUCTION BY DAVE ANDERSON

Photographs from the Magnum archive by Abbas, Bryn Campbell, Elliott Erwitt, Philippe Halsman, Thomas Hoepker, Danny Lyon, Roger Malloch, and Alex Webb

Harry N. Abrams, Inc., Publishers

Frontispiece: Thomas Hoepker, Muhammad Ali, 1966 (detail)


Editor: Christopher Sweet
Editorial Assistant: Sigi Nacson
Designer: Peter Buchanan-Smith
Design Assistant: Lindsay Ballant
Production Managers: Stanley Redfern and Norman Watkins


Library of Congress Cataloging-in-Publication Data

Muhammad Ali / by Magnum photographers ; introduction by Dave Anderson.
    p. cm.
 Includes bibliographical references and index.
 ISBN 0-8109-5605-5 (hardcover)
 1. Ali, Muhammad, 1942- 2. Boxers (Sports)—United States—Biography. I. Magnum Photos, inc.

 GV1132.A4A29 2004
 796.83'092—dc22

2004008775

Printed and bound in China

10 9 8 7 6 5 4 3 2 1

Harry N. Abrams, Inc.
100 Fifth Avenue
New York, N.Y. 10011
www.abramsbooks.com

Abrams is a subsidiary of

**INTRODUCTION BY DAVE ANDERSON** / The dull mask of Parkinson's syndrome that Muhammad Ali wears now is not the face remembered by anyone who knew him when.

When that face changed every few seconds.

When that face was laughing. Glaring. Staring. Posing. Meditating. Praying. Clowning. Preening. Boxing. Training. Sweating. Flirting with a woman who would become his second wife. Listening. Joking. Jiving. Cooing. When that face was simply being Muhammad Ali, the one and only.

That's the beauty of all these Magnum photos. They remind us of the years when that ever changing face was so familiar to millions, maybe billions. That face that always will be familiar to anyone who remembers it.

The first time I saw that face up close was in 1963, before the young boxer then known as Cassius Clay would fight in Madison Square Garden for the first time. His opponent would be Doug Jones, but that up-and-coming boyish face was the attraction, and I was to interview him in his hotel room. When I knocked on the door, it swung open and that face suddenly towered above me, fists raised.

"Pow, pow, pow," that face barked as he danced side to side, his left jabs stopping inches from my face. "Pow, pow."

Just as quickly, that face relaxed in a smile. We sat down and talked for half an hour. For nearly two decades, as a sportswriter for the *New York Times* and earlier for the *New York Journal-American*, I wrote about more than thirty of his fights, traveling to wherever that face, often half-hidden under a towel or in the hood of a white satin bathrobe, was about to appear in a boxing ring.

That face of a three-time world heavyweight champion was so familiar, it didn't need a boxing ring to be recognized.

Two years after Ali's last fight, my wife Maureen was having lunch at an outdoor cafe in Athens, Greece, when the bill arrived. As she opened her wallet, the waiter standing near her couldn't help but notice one of our family's favorite snapshots—our daughter Jean Marie next to that familiar face in a white terry-cloth bathrobe after a training-camp workout.

"Ali!" the waiter shrieked. "Ali! Ali!"

What other face would prompt such delighted recognition halfway around the world from that face's home? The Pope? Probably, but not necessarily. A famous politician? Maybe, maybe not, depending on where in the world you were.

That face transcended boxing.

Ali usually fought in the United States but he also fought in Toronto, London, Frankfurt, Zurich, Tokyo, Vancouver, Dublin, Jakarta, Kinshasa, Kuala Lumpur, Manila, San Juan, Munich, and Nassau where that face was as familiar as it was in New York or Las Vegas. For two decades, beginning when he won an Olympic gold medal as Cassius Clay in Rome in 1960, that face was telecast worldwide and that face was in newspapers and magazines worldwide.

That face appealed to the peasants as much as, if not more than, it did to the powerful.

And when Ali, as a devout Muslim who had "nothin' against them Viet Cong," refused to be drafted into the United States military in 1967 and was exiled by boxing authorities for three and one-half years, that face appealed all the more to those who protested the Vietnam War and respected his stand, just as it annoyed those who supported that war. But the boxer in that face may have never been the same.

"The shame," his longtime trainer, Angelo Dundee, once said, alluding to that exile, "is that we never saw Muhammad at his best."

Dundee, his greatest admirer but also his most knowledgeable critic, contends that Ali would have been at his best sometime between early 1967, when he was stripped of the title he had snatched from Sonny Liston on February 25, 1964, and late 1970, when boxing authorities allowed him to resume his career. But the exile for having refused induction, Dundee acknowledged, had its advantages.

"When he came back," Dundee once recalled, "he was stronger. The maturity was there."

Not right away. On March 8, 1971, he lost a unanimous 15-round decision to Joe Frazier in a Garden spectacle, his first defeat. Three months later the United States Supreme Court upheld his right to refuse military duty. In a 12-round loss to Ken Norton in 1973, he suffered a broken jaw. But on October 30, 1974, in a bout that started at four o'clock in the morning in Zaire in order to bring the closed-circuit telecast to New York at ten o'clock the night before, he regained the title with a stunning 8th-round knockout of George Foreman.

Suddenly that face glowed again. Ali was the heavyweight champion again.

Nearly a year later, on October 1, 1975, in Manila, that face was weary. It had survived 14 brutal rounds with Joe Frazier, whose manager, Eddie Futch, stopped the fight because Frazier couldn't see out of his left eye. Even though Ali won, he needed nearly an hour to gather his strength before meeting reporters in the interview area. What had the fight been like?

"Next to death," Ali said.

That face was never quite the same after that. Ali kept winning until losing the title in 1978 to young Leon Spinks in a 15-round decision; then he regained the title in a rematch, but after a brief retirement, he looked old and tired against Larry Holmes in Las Vegas until his manager, Herbert Muhammad, signaled Dundee to throw in the towel. KO by 11.

Soon the Parkinson's mask began to warp that face. When it smiled, those who knew him from before noticed the mischief in his eyes but that face would never be what it was. Never what all these photos prove it was.

**PHILIPPE HALSMAN /**
Cassius Marcellus Clay, 1963

# LONDON/1966

**BRYN CAMPBELL** / Muhammad Ali leaves the weigh-in prior to his fight with Henry Cooper

10

**BRYN CAMPBELL** / Ali training for the Cooper fight in a Hampstead gym

**BRYN CAMPBELL** / Ali training for his fight with Henry Cooper

15

**BRYN CAMPBELL /**
World Heavyweight Champion Muhammad Ali
shaking hands with challenger Henry Cooper at the
weigh-in before their title fight on May 21, 1966, at
Arsenal Stadium. They had fought before in 1963. Ali
won both fights, but in the first fight Cooper had
dropped then Cassius Clay with a hard left.

THOMAS HOEPKER / Ali praying to Allah before the first round of his title fight against Brian London on August 6, 1966, at Earl's Court

(overleaf left) **BRYN CAMPBELL** / Ali landing a hard right to Brian London's jaw

(overleaf right) **THOMAS HOEPKER** / Ali celebrating his third-round knockout victory over Brian London

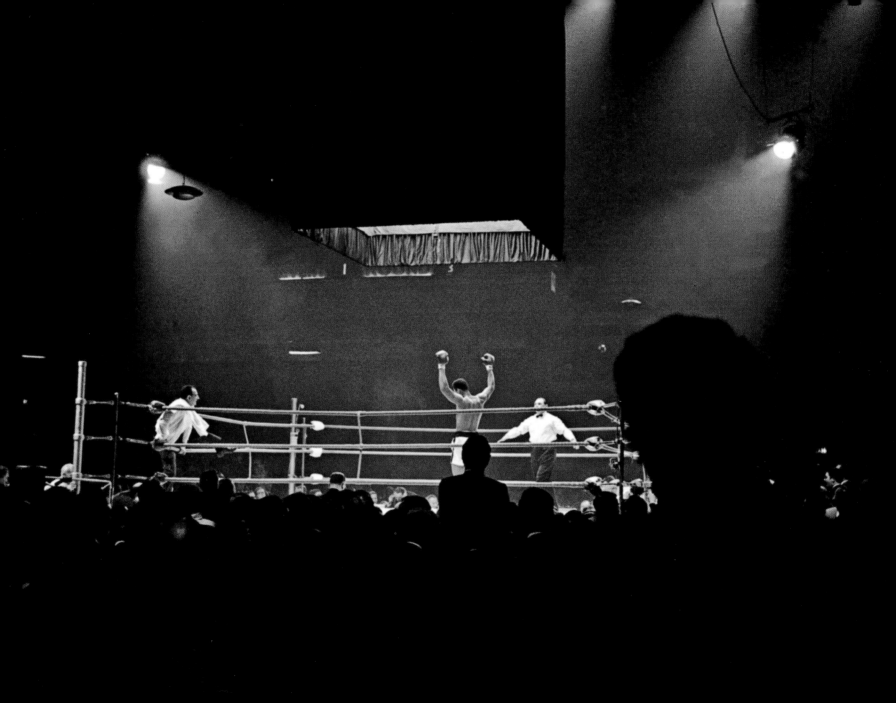

**THOMAS HOEPKER** / Driving to the gym

**THOMAS HOEPKER** / Ali in pre-fight training

**THOMAS HOEPKER** / Ali in pre-fight training

24

**THOMAS HOEPKER** / With his brother Rahaman (Rudolph Clay) at his London hotel

**THOMAS HOEPKER** / After a fight, Ali always treated himself to a big bowl of ice cream

**THOMAS HOEPKER /**
In his hotel room prior to the Brian London fight

28

**THOMAS HOEPKER** / Ali in a restaurant with his manager Herbert Muhammad, the son of Black Muslim leader Elijah Muhammad

**THOMAS HOEPKER** / Ali is fitted for a new suit by a tailor on London's Savile Row

(opposite) **THOMAS HOEPKER** / With Mrs. Gordon Parks at a dinner in a London restaurant

**THOMAS HOEPKER** / With football star/actor Jim Brown on the set of the film The Dirty Dozen

(opposite) **THOMAS HOEPKER** / Frightened by a bee while visiting the set of The Dirty Dozen

# LOUISVILLE/1966

**THOMAS HOEPKER** / Ali visiting his hometown of Louisville, Kentucky

34

**THOMAS HOEPKER** / Standing in front of his high school near an Army recruitment poster. At the time, Ali had refused to be drafted into the military.

**THOMAS HOEPKER** / Ali's parents, Cassius and Odessa Clay, at their home in Louisville

**THOMAS HOEPKER** / Being driven around his hometown

# CHICAGO/1966

**ROGER** MALLOCH / A Nation of Islam meeting

**THOMAS HOEPKER** / Talking with Nation of Islam sisters outside Southside Muslim Temple

**ROGER MALLOCH** / At a Nation of Islam meeting

**THOMAS HOEPKER** / Visiting with Nation of Islam leader Elijah Muhammad in his Chicago home

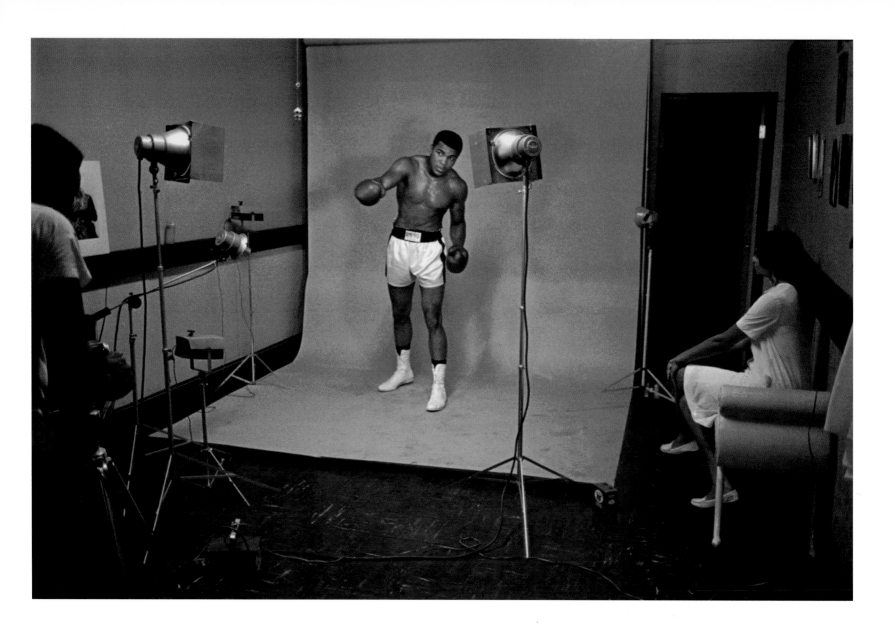

**THOMAS HOEPKER** / Posing for promotional pictures at Herbert Muhammad's photo studio

**THOMAS HOEPKER** / In a bakery shop flirting with Belinda Boyd, who would later become his second wife

**THOMAS HOEPKER** / At the Museum of Science and Industry 48

**THOMAS HOEPKER** / Strolling under the elevated railroad in downtown Chicago

**THOMAS HOEPKER** / Drawing a crowd on Chicago's South Side

**THOMAS HOEPKER** / In front of the Commodities Exchange

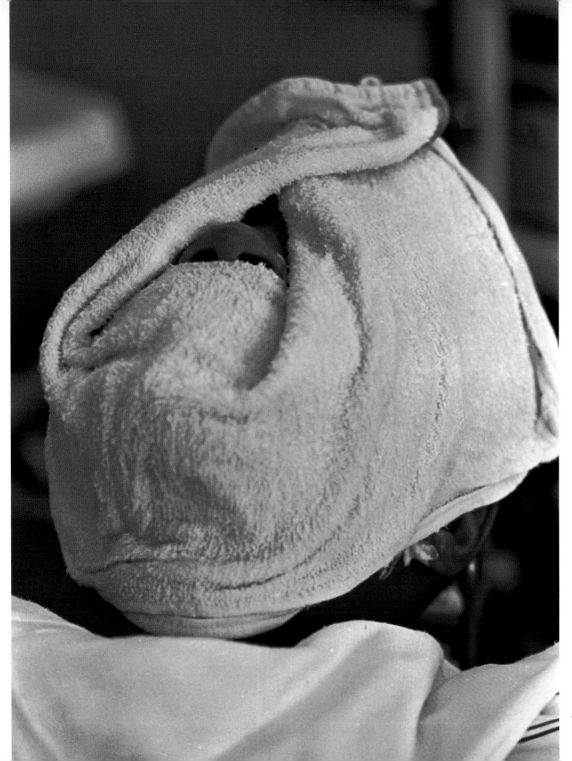

**THOMAS HOEPKER /**
Having a facial and a shave in a South Side barbershop      54

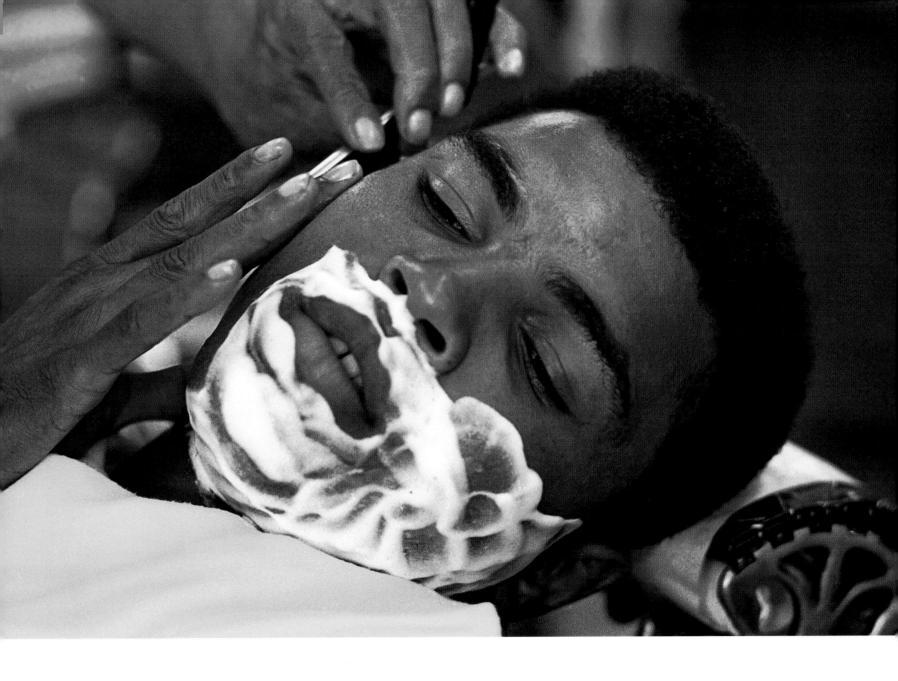

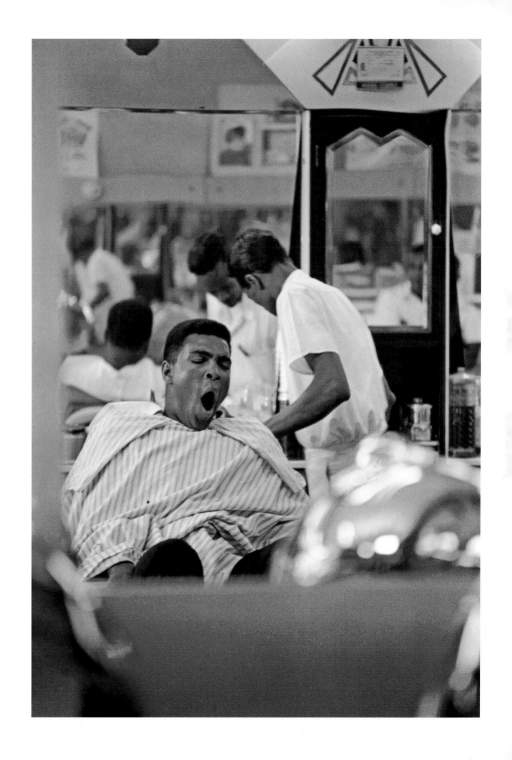

57

**THOMAS HOEPKER** / Studying himself in the mirror

**THOMAS HOEPKER** / Out on the town

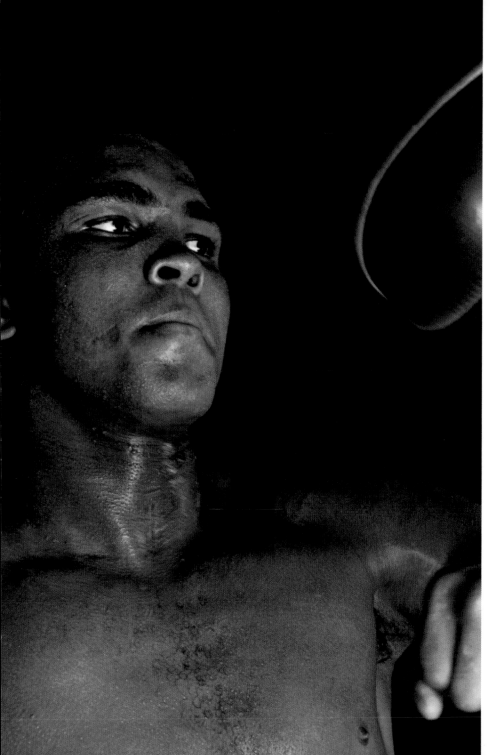

**THOMAS HOEPKER** / Training on the speedbag                    62

**THOMAS HOEPKER /**
Then world heavyweight champion Muhammad Ali talking to Johnny Coulon,
the world bantamweight champion of 1915, in his Chicago gym

**THOMAS HOEPKER** / Taking a break

**THOMAS HOEPKER** / In gym training

**THOMAS HOEPKER** / A left and a right on a bridge over the Chicago River

**THOMAS HOEPKER** / On a bridge over the Chicago River

# MIAMI/1970

**DANNY LYON** / At the Embers Steak House

**THOMAS HOEPKER** / In front of his new fast-food restaurant "Champ Burger"

**THOMAS HOEPKER** / Inside "Champ Burger"

**THOMAS HOEPKER** / Ali engaged in a mock alley fight with a fan

**THOMAS HOEPKER** / The "fight" continues outside Chris Dundee's gym in Miami Beach

**THOMAS HOEPKER** / In Miami Beach while training for his upcoming fight against Jerry Quarry

**DANNY LYON** / After an early morning run

**DANNY LYON** / After an early morning run

**DANNY LYON** / Training for the Jerry Quarry fight

**DANNY LYON** / Outside his training camp

**DANNY LYON** / Reciting poetry to the photographer

**DANNY LYON** / Spectators at the Fifth Street Gym watching Muhammad Ali train for his fight with Jerry Quarry

**DANNY LYON** / Photographs of boxers on the wall of the Fifth Street Gym

(overleaf) **THOMAS HOEPKER** / Training in Chris Dundee's Fifth Street Gym

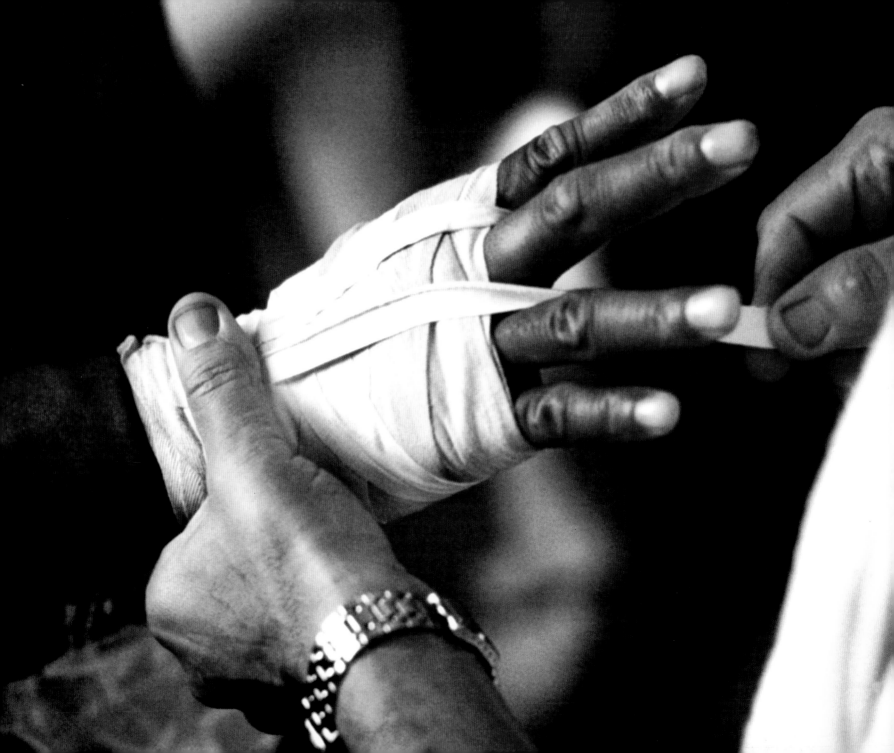

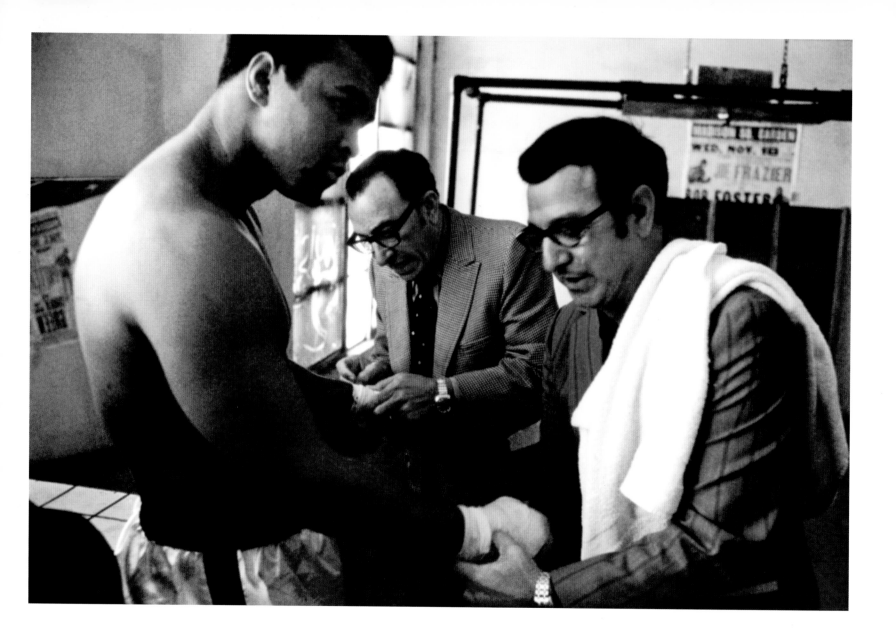

**THOMAS HOEPKER** / Chris and Angelo Dundee wrapping Ali's hands

**THOMAS HOEPKER** / Working the heavy bag at Dundee's gym

**THOMAS HOEPKER** / Working the speedbag

**DANNY LYON** / In the ring at Chris Dundee's gym

**THOMAS HOEPKER** / Doing sit ups

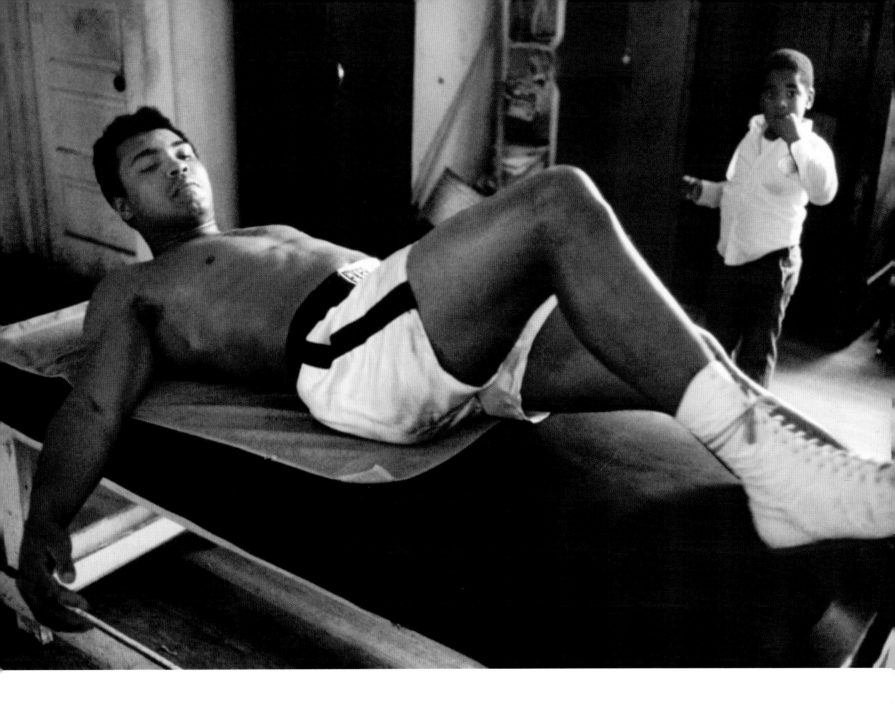

**THOMAS HOEPKER** / Getting a rub down

**THOMAS HOEPKER** / Training at Chris Dundee's gym

**THOMAS HOEPKER** / Skipping rope before a mirror

**THOMAS HOEPKER** / Reading a fan letter

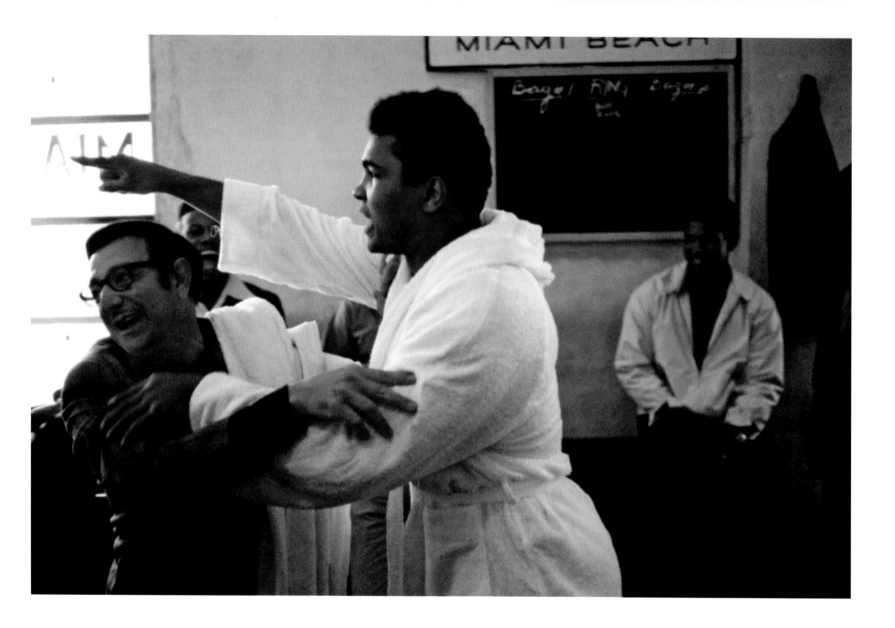

**THOMAS HOEPKER** / *Ali clowning with his trainer, Angelo Dundee*

**THOMAS HOEPKER /**
Talking to the fans while training
at Chris Dundee's gym

(overleaf left)
**THOMAS HOEPKER /**
Still life, boxing gear in the gym
(overleaf right)
**THOMAS HOEPKER /**
Ali's left fist

**PHILADELPHIA/1970**

**THOMAS HOEPKER** / Muhammad and Belinda Ali's home in Philadelphia

116

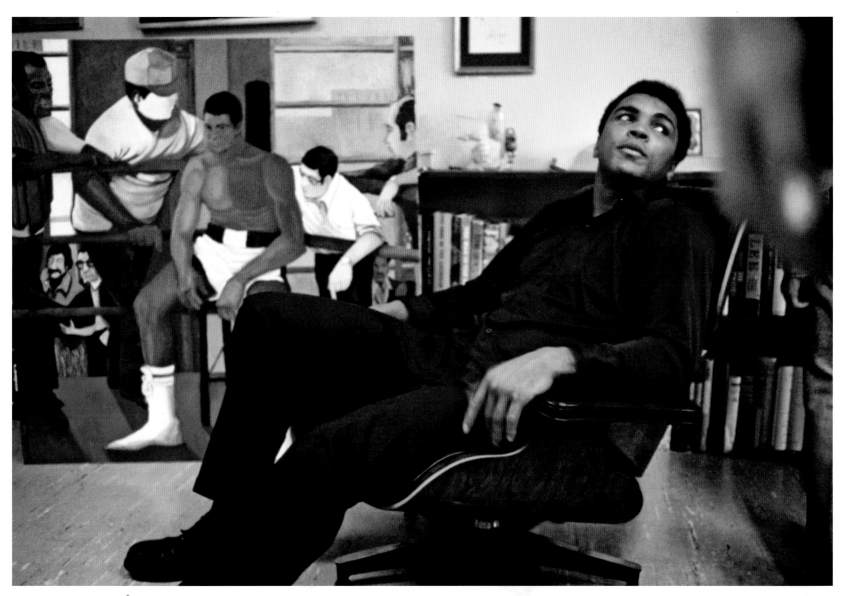

**THOMAS HOEPKER** / Ali at home

**THOMAS HOEPKER** / Ali and his wife Blinda in their home

**THOMAS HOEPKER** / Belinda Ali and children at home

# NEW YORK

**ELLIOTT ERWITT** / Joe Frazier and Muhammad Ali, Madison Square Garden, New York, March 8, 1971. Ali would lose by decision, his first loss.

**ALEX WEBB** / At the 369th Regiment Armory in Harlem for a speaking engagement, December 9, 1974

**ALEX WEBB** / Refereeing a lightweight fight at Saint Mary's Recreation Center, December 9, 1974

**ALEX WEBB** / Refereeing a lightweight fight at Saint Mary's Recreation Center, December 9, 1974

# KINSHASA/1974

**ABBAS** / Ali with Zaire's President Mobutu Sese Seko at a reception given by the president in his palace by the Congo River

**ABBAS** / Ali and his mother Odessa in Kinshasa, Zaire, October 1974

**ABBAS** / A poster announcing the world heavyweight championship fight between defending champion George Foreman and Muhammad Ali on October 30, 1974

**ABBAS** / Ali fooling around with fans and the press

(these and preceeding pages) **ABBAS** / Ali at his training camp before the Foreman fight

ABBAS

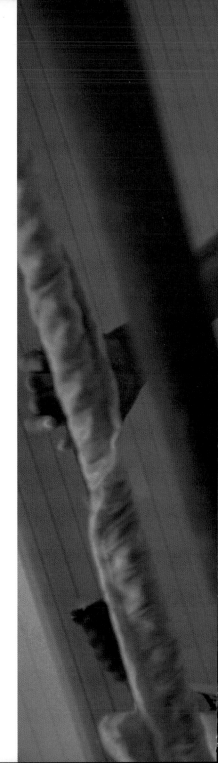

**ABBAS** / Ali with Zaire's President Mobutu

**ABBAS** / At the stadium, spectators and soldiers standing under a portrait of President Mobutu

**ABBAS** / Ali about to be weighed before the start of the fight

**ABBAS** / The former world heavyweight champion Joe Frazier in the audience

**ABBAS** / Ali avoiding a blow from George Foreman

**ABBAS** / Ali and Foreman battling late in the fight

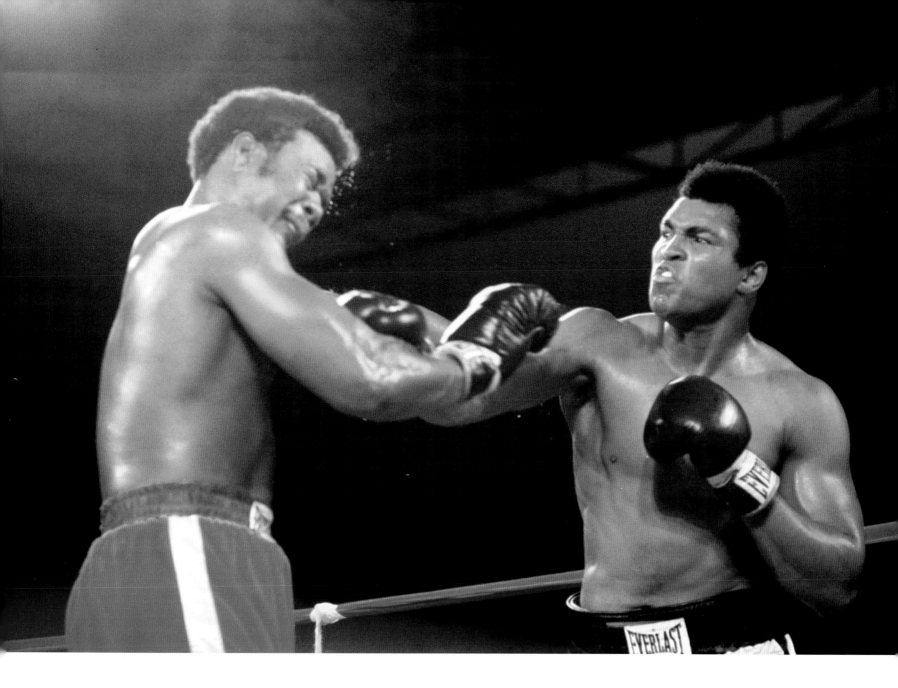

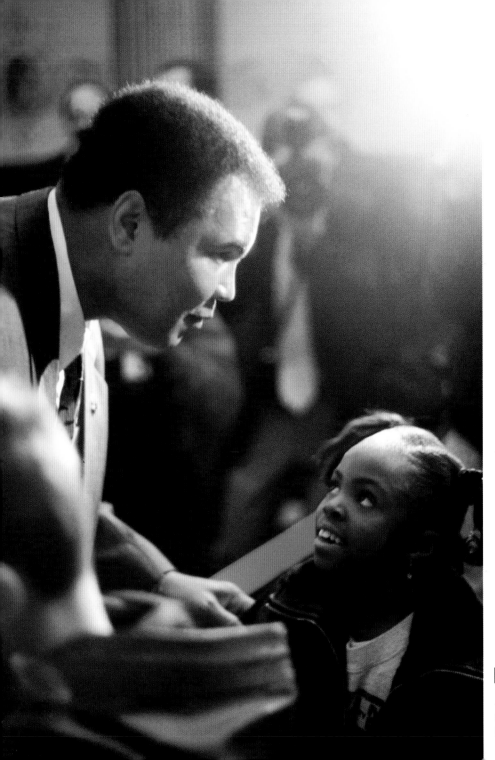

# MICHIGAN/1997

**THOMAS HOEPKER /**
Visiting the State Capitol in Lansing, Michigan, where he was
being honored for his work with children

152

**THOMAS HOEPKER** / In a limousine returning home from his visit to Lansing